Marvelous
Predictions

Marvelous Predictions

Willie Wright, Sr.

authorHOUSE®

AuthorHouse™
1663 Liberty Drive
Bloomington, IN 47403
www.authorhouse.com
Phone: 1-800-839-8640

First published by AuthorHouse   11/03/2011

ISBN: 978-1-4670-9429-0 (sc)
ISBN: 978-1-4670-9426-9 (ebk)

Printed in the United States of America

This book is dedicated

to my wife and family

Contents

Introduction

The following is a collection of true stories that will amaze you. These true stories actually materialized at the beginning of my life, during my childhood days, when I was five years old, and continued to the present day of 2009. Each segment in the book will encourage you to continue reading until completion of the book.

These true stories superseded the famous Jean Dixon's percentage ratings of accurate predictions. To be frank, I have a 100% rating ever since I began to predict at an early age.

The reason for documenting these marvelous predictions is to let the whole world know that such prophecy is real and that there are people who have these individual recognizable gifts.

Witnesses have accounted for every prediction I've made in the past seventy years. These persons were told in plenty of time before the actual moment of each circumstance that would happen, sometimes as long as one and half months before the event and sometimes closer to the occurrence.

Many persons say that they don't believe unless they see or witness something on their own. So I decided to eliminate the segment of unbelievers by letting them witness the truth, thus making them believers that these amazing episodes of prophecy were really true.

These prophecies would come to me, no matter where I might have been, at any time. I really did not go seeking for the answers because the answers would be made known to me by means of supernatural power, God.

I want to remind you that each event related in this book came to me at any time and anywhere unexpectedly. Each event was a true connection.

Relax and continue to read this book in its entirety because you will then understand the continuation of so many accurate predictions by me.

As a Young Boy

I was born in Williamston, South Carolina on November 24, 1937 to my parents, Sadie and Willie Wright. They were wonderful parents who were considerate, caring, loving, religious, and hard working.

My mother taught elementary school in School District 1 in Williamston, Anderson County, South Carolina which is known as the Palmetto State. It is a small town, but a more relaxing and comfortable place than many towns and cities in the United States of America.

My mother obtained her first teaching position in the public school system, at a school located across the street from where she lived in Williamston. That school was named Caroline Elementary and High School, which included grades one through twelve. The closeness of the school to her home was very fortunate for her because of the fact she did not have to drive or travel to work in a vehicle.

My mother taught elementary school before I was born. After teaching for a short while, she met and married my father, Willie Wright.

When I was a pre-school child, my grandmother, Mattie Lou Sizer, operated a variety candy store across the street in front of Caroline Elementary and High School.

As a young child, not old enough to attend school, on many a day I would stand in the front yard of our home between the store and hedges near the street. Of course, there was a gate and fence on the front yard. The reason for the gate and fence was to make sure that I would not venture into the street where there was danger of vehicles traveling to and fro.

There were many times that I would stand or sit on my bicycle or tricycle near the gate to watch the various activities being held outside of the school building on the schoolyard and playground.

When I reached the age of five, I had certain beliefs. One of those beliefs was that "there was no such thing as a ghost." Walking or being in a cemetery at night, or in places some people would claim to be haunted, was not a ghostly problem for me at this young age.

But on one cold December night when I was five years old, I was sleeping in my grandmother's house, which was

100 years old, when something transpired. My mother and father were also living in this old house during this time.

In the middle of the night, with the bedcover pulled up over me to my shoulders to keep me warm, I went to sleep. All lights were turned off for the night. Later in the night during the black of darkness, a most memorable moment came when I felt someone gradually pulling the cover off me, from my shoulder downward toward my feet.

To my astonishment, I looked up to see what was going on and at that moment realized that it was not my parents moving the bedcover. I saw a ghostly figure in the form of a human being kneeling on the right side of my bed staring at me. The head, shoulders and the rest of the upper body were clearly visible to me. At that moment I knew, without a doubt, who was physically removing my bed cover at a slow pace. It was a "GHOST." This sighting in darkness had the distinction of being described as "whitish in form" with a human appearance.

A short while after realizing what was present beside my bed, I decided to call my parents and ask them if they came into my room and pulled the bedcover off me. They said, "No". Of course, I already knew the answer. My parents, after answering my question, said that they were asleep and were not aware of anything until I told them.

From that moment of seeing a "ghost", and actually experiencing this real episode of the presence of a "ghost", experiences of prophecy began to noticeably occur, being true each time.

I really believe that this "ghost" was God. My reason for saying this is that ever since that December night I have made many predictions, all of them coming to me in an instant, and all in advance of each happening, and all being 100 % true. I would say that it is the work of "God". He was working and continues to work through me with these prophecies with pinpoint accuracy, including exact times.

My grandmother's house burned down, but my memory of this event still lives on.

Blaze, High Winds Win Over Firemen

Bus Supervisor

During the early years of my marriage, in the 60s and 70s, I decided to sign up for school bus training, in order to supplement my income by driving a school bus for the local high school in my town of Williamston, SC.

My school bus supervisor was David, who owned a theater in Anderson at the Market Place. We bus drivers would get our paychecks by going to the local high school once a month to receive our compensation for the month.

One morning when it was time to go and pick up my check, something came to me in my mind at that moment and said that David would bring my check to my house personally. I would not have to go and pick it up this time. Within the next 60 seconds, an automobile arrived in my yard and the horn blew while the automobile was sitting in my driveway. I went and opened my house door and went outside.

To my astonishment, there was David, the school bus supervisor. As I approached the vehicle, I told David that something came to me and told me about 60 seconds ago that he would deliver my paycheck to me at home this morning. David was amazed and astonished to hear me say what was going to happen in advance. He gave me my check and I thanked him for delivering it to me. He departed wondering how a person could predict in advance what was going to happen with accuracy.

My accuracy rating at this time continued to be 100%. This prediction came about 60 seconds before it happened. Anytime and anywhere when that something came to me, predictions would always come true.

At Preacher's Home

One day, my wife and I decided to go over to her sister Geraldine's house, which was located across town in Williamston. Geraldine was married to Rev. Spurgeon, Jr.

After being there for a while, and as I was sitting on the couch in the living room, something came to me and said that I could predict the arrival of Cousin Mattie and her husband Robert precisely within a minute in a certain hour.

Robert and Mattie lived in Pendleton, SC. The distance from Pendleton to Williamston is approximately 15 miles. I told everyone present that Robert and Mattie would open the kitchen door at 4:20 pm today, or within 60 seconds of that specified time (the exact minute and hour).

An electric clock was running and hanging on the wall above my head. It had a second hand on it, denoting seconds within each minute. Everyone was astonished and amazed to hear me predict something like that. I kept my eye on the clock.

As the time approached 4:20 pm, I got the attention of everyone so that we could all see if my prediction would come true. Everyone got quiet and we were all watching the clock.

When the long hand on the clock got to 4:20 pm, I then emphasized that within 60 seconds of that minute Robert and Mattie would turn the doorknob of the side door of the kitchen and walk inside. Of course, we all had not expected them to visit during this time of day.

The second hand on the clock had just reached 12 at 4:20 pm, thus making the next 60 seconds crucial for a prediction of specific accuracy.

The seconds continued to run and approached the 40-second mark on the clock when suddenly the knob on the side door slowly started turning. There were Mattie and Robert entering the house precisely at time I had predicted.

All in the living room were amazed and astonished as they witnessed how I could predict with complete accuracy in a timely setting.

It is almost unimaginable how I can be anywhere at anytime when something can come to me instantly and tell me what is going to happen and how it is going to happen and be so precise.

Some people don't believe until they can actually see something for themselves. Well, I have a lot of believers!

At Workplace

There have been several predictions made by me at my workplace, Roadway Express, Inc., a trucking company in Greenville, SC.

This specific prediction began while I was sitting in the dock office working. After turning my head and looking out the window to my right, I saw a dockworker attempting to remove some freight from inside the trailer, what is called the "nose" of the trailer, that was sitting backed up to the dock. I heard Jack, a dock supervisor, tell the dockworker to weigh those three pieces of sizeable freight that had to be moved by a tow-motor because of their size and weight. The weighing scales were situated directly in front of my office window.

Suddenly, something came to me in my mind and told me what would be the total weight of all three pieces of freight. Immediately, I went outside of the dock office and approached Jack. He was standing beside the dock scales waiting for the freight to be weighed. I told Jack that something came to me and told me exactly what the total weight of the three pieces would be. He replied, "Really?"

I told Jack to get a pen and write down on paper the predicted weight. I wanted him to write the weight himself, not me, to prove a point of accuracy. I told him to write 1727 lbs. as a total sum for the three pieces to be weighed. "Jack,

I want you to do the adding yourself, not me." He added the weight of each piece. I asked Jack what was the total weight. Jack said, "Willie, that is exactly the same total you gave me before the freight was weighed. It is amazing!"

I then told Jack that I really wanted to see if another prediction of mine would come true. In this case, I wanted him to actually see if I was right. Well, this is actually another example of predicting with 100% accuracy.

Employees Excitement

While working at Roadway Express as a Density Coordinator, part of my job was to inspect freight for correct labeling, weight, forward destinations, as well as correct descriptions on freight bills, etc.

After reporting to work on one particular morning at 4:00 am, I began to make my walk around the dock looking at and checking freight bills at each dock stand near each trailer parked at the outbound dock. When leaving my first trailer and then going to the next trailer, I noticed an overhead light was off. As I walked under the light, it lit up and stayed on. I didn't pay much attention, but remembered what had happened to the light that particular morning.

The next morning after reporting to work, I started my routine of walking around the dock from trailer to trailer. Further down the dock I noticed an overhead light off and not burning. I remembered what happened to the light that was off yesterday morning. So this time I was curious about the light being out. I decided to walk under the light to see what would happen. After walking under the light that was off, this particular light immediately came back on in a few seconds. This started to become exciting!

As a matter of fact, every day when I saw a light "off", I would go and walk under the overhead light. It would come on each and every time, no matter where it was located on the dock.

Some of the dockworkers would approach me when they noticed a light off and not burning. They would ask me to walk over under the light and cause it to come on without touching any switch or anything.

The news started spreading around the freight terminal about the special "feats" of mine, turning on lights without touching a switch. It was not only amazing to me, but to the dockworkers also. They mentioned the fact that it must be something special about me. They had never seen anyone do such a thing before.

Several days later, I was beginning my 4:00 am shift. As I was walking down the steps from my new office to start my tour of duty on the dock, I heard Mike, the terminal operations manager call me over to where he was standing. Immediately I wondered what he wanted.

Mike told me that he had heard from various persons that I could turn "off-lights" back on again. Then he pointed across the dock to a light that was off at the time. He asked me to go over and see if I could turn that light back on without touching anything. I said, "Okay, be glad to do it." Mike wanted to see for himself if what he had heard about me is really true.

So I walked over and stood under the specific off-light pointed out by him. The light came on immediately. I turned around and walked back to where Mike was standing. I told him that the mission was accomplished. The light is "on" and that was what he really wanted to witness himself. He reacted with unbelief and astonishment at what he had just seen with his own eyes.

Mike saw for himself what happened with his own eyes. This was another example of the wonders to perform with amazing results.

Community Center Amazement

In the town of Williamston, there is a school building that once was named Caroline Elementary and High School. After new and additional schools were built in the local area, this school was eliminated and later became a community center in the town.

I was elected to a position of Vice-President on the Board of Directors. This organization, known as the WACC (Williamston Action Community Club) receives its support from citizens in the local and surrounding communities. We have scheduled monthly meeting at the Caroline Community Center.

On this particular meeting day, being at nighttime and having to use lights, one of the ladies who attended the meeting approached me. She said, "There is a light on the left side in the front of the building that has not come on for several days. We need to call the electric power company (Duke Power) to see if they can fix it."

At that moment, I thought about all the times at Roadway Express, Inc. in Greenville, when lights would come on as I walked under them. So I told the lady, Sallie that I would go over to where the light was off and see about it. I went to the light and stood under it for a few seconds.

Shortly, I turned to walk back where Sallie was standing. When I looked back over my left shoulder toward the light, I saw that the light had come on. I told her that I appreciated her informing me about the "off-light". Sallie was amazed and astonished at seeing the light come on before her own eyes. I told her that we saved time by not calling Duke Power Electric Co. concerning the light.

For many days later, I would always check by the community center to see if the light continued to burn and this light continued to burn.

Thanks to that something about me that make things happen. It is amazing! I have never seen anything like this before!

Communication with Dispatcher

When working in the dock offices at Roadway Express, Inc., both inbound and outbound offices had bulletin boards displaying truck drivers and their times of arrival at the terminal.

One day, after an incoming truckload of freight had not arrived, something told me to call the dispatcher at the other end of the terminal. Gene was the line-haul dispatcher during this particular shift of work. I called him on the telephone and told him that a specific truckload was overdue. I asked him to look through his office window to see if the overdue driver was entering the doorway. Gene said the driver was arriving during the moment while I was speaking and that he was checking in.

For one and a half weeks, on a constant daily basis, I would call Gene and tell him when each driver should be checking in at the terminal with him. Each time I was right.

One time when I called Gene, he said the particular truck driver was not at the window checking in at his office. I immediately told Gene to look out through his window at the entrance door, because the driver should be approaching this dispatch window. Gene said, "You are right, because the driver is now walking in the entrance door and approaching my window as we speak".

This specific timing to the where-abouts of truck drivers continued for about two weeks without error on my part until I stopped calling him.

Why was I so accurate so many times? It was because something told me instantly, in my mind, the location of each overdue driver. These locations were accurate within a time frame of only 60 seconds. My predictions would always come true.

It is again amazing and astonishing!

Accident on Job

It seems as though many things happened unexpectedly at Roadway Express, Inc. Employees moved into a newly built trucking terminal located in Greenville, which was more than twice the size of the old terminal that was located near Bob Jones University and the Shriner's Hospital in the city of Greenville.

Being a Dock Records Clerk at the time, there were times when I had to make a trip around the dock at each trailer loading door with my tally cart, calculator and other necessities. My job was to keep up to date with the bills and amount of weight loaded on each trailer and to make sure that each shipment of freight was correctly loaded to its proper destination on the newly built dock. We had what was called a "drag-line". This line had carts constantly moving around the dock loaded with freight destined for many places throughout the United States and other countries.

I had just begun to tally freight at one of the loading doors at the dock, which was situated at the side of the entrance to the trailer. I was standing with my back to the trailer, head down looking at the paperwork on the cart. The drag-line was running. All of a sudden, I heard a tow-motor from the opposite side of the dock. The gas pedal was pressed down and it was speeding across the dock.

Unaware of what was going on, the driver on the tow-motor had a long rug on the pole of his tow-motor headed toward the trailer where I was standing. The driver had not raised the rug to the proper level of height, so that it would be above the moving carts while going between carts on the drag-line. Instead, he had the rug pole low while trying to move between the moving carts on the drag-line that had only short spaces between the floats.

All of a sudden, something hit my tally cart and knocked me and the tally cart off the dock down into the trailer yard below, with paperwork and everything else airborne. As I was trying to recover off the ground, I noticed a bruise on my left shoulder. I had been knocked backward with my shoulder hitting a steel-beam support, thus avoiding hitting my head, which would have caused severe injury and disaster.

It was God that prevented harmful injury to me, or even death, at Roadway. Thanks be to God!

Miracle at Trailer Yard

At Roadway Express, Inc., as a part of my job, I was assigned to do a periodic yard check of trailers to see if there was any unknown freight that did not have any paperwork. There was a rule that any rear door on a trailer that was open on the yard had to be pulled down and closed. To do this, I would have to climb up on the rear of the trailer and stand up to reach the cord on the back door, in order to pull or close the door.

One day, while I was out in the yard checking, a door was open. So I climbed up on the trailer and reached up to grab the cord above with my back to the yard. The cord slipped out of my hand and suddenly I was falling backward out of the trailer, with several feet to go before hitting the ground, which was asphalt.

Some way and somehow, with "God on my side", I descended toward the ground backward. While I was in the air for that short period of time, my body made a 180-degree turn, positioning my body to hit the ground with my face down and not the back of my head. With this force, I still hit my mouth on the asphalt, causing me some loose teeth and bleeding.

After getting my breath, I managed my way back up on the dock and reported this to the operations manager,

Jim. Of course, I went to the emergency room at Greenville Memorial Hospital to be treated.

I thank God for guiding me to the ground with a rotation of 180 degrees. I continue to be amazed how God saved me from severe injury or possible death.

While Traveling in Truck

There are several radio stations people can dial into, depending on which one is their favorite. It may be one that gives the current news, plays your favorite music, tells jokes, or whatever the station has to broadcast.

Most of the time, I chose to, dial in on the radio station WRIX in Anderson, SC. Here I could listen to news and music and hear commentaries. Sometimes, I would hear questions that the public could answer by dialing a specific telephone number that would be given out to listeners.

On this particular day, with my cellular phone by my side, I was listening to radio station WRIX. During these moments of listening, as I usually do when driving, there were questions being asked. Anyone in radio land could call into the radio station to give the answer, if they knew the answer to the question or questions.

One question that was asked was, "What was the lowest temperature ever recorded on Grandfather Mountain?" Frankly, I did not know the answer at that particular moment. I knew the telephone number for call-ins and I also had a cell phone to make the call, if I knew the answer to the question.

All of a sudden, something came to my mind and told me to call in to the radio station and tell them the answer is minus 32 degrees Fahrenheit. I immediately dialed the telephone, hoping that no one had answered the question before my contact with the radio station. Fortunately, no one had answered the question correctly.

The person at the radio station asked me for my answer. I told him what the answer was. He asked me how I knew the answer. I replied, "The answer came to me. Something came to me in my mind giving me the answer to call in and win the prize to be given away."

The radio announcer seemed to be in somewhat of a daze or astonishment as to how I knew the answer. He told me that the answer was correct, and that I could come by the radio station and pick up my prize at any time. Since I was in the Anderson area, I decided to drive by and pick up my prize, which I did in the next 30 minutes.

This was another example of how things would come to me in my mind, directing or telling me what is or what is to be. This was one of many times this sort of thing has happened with accuracy.

Amazing! Amazing! That is what it is! That is why I want the world to know how these predictions come true. Thanks be to God.

Visions and Answers

On the way to work early one morning to start my 6:00 am shift, there were very interesting moments on the way. When I was only 2.2 miles from my destination, a marvelous thing occurred.

A lighted neon sign suddenly appeared ahead and in front of me. On this lighted sign, there were three names, with only one name in bright light, whereas the other two names were listed in plain sight with a darkness of shade over them. The name "Sam" stood out with a brightness, which made it very distinguishable from the other two.

At this time, Sam was the terminal operations manager (T.O.M). He was one of three candidates who were seeking a job as sales representative at Monroe, NC, which was a satellite or branch of Roadway Express, Inc. in Greenville.

During the following days, practically everyone at Roadway was debating as to who was going to be selected for that sales job in Monroe, NC. Actually, no one knew, but only tried to guess who it might be.

After reporting to work that morning, I told my fellow workers that I knew in advance the person who would actually be selected and get the job. Everyone asked me how I knew. I told them that something came and appeared before me that morning on the way to work. My co-workers asked me to tell who it might be. I responded by telling them that I would not reveal the answer until a few days before the selection.

As days passed, I just listened to my co-workers talk about the selection. As for me, I had already predicted the selection of the job, but kept it to myself. After all, I wanted to see if another prediction of mine would come true.

Sam tried to get me to tell him in advance who would be the elected choice, but I refused to even give him the answer.

My work-shift during this time was what was called "7 on and 7 off". That is, on this schedule a person would work 7 days and be off the next 7 days. Each workday would consist of 12 working hours. My last shift during the week before selection was on a Sunday, before going on a week's break. The selection was to be made on the following Thursday.

I decided, on my last workday of the week preceding the selection on the next Thursday, to reveal the answer. It was approximately an hour before the end of the shift when

I approached Sam in the office. I reached out to shake his hand, congratulating him on being selected for the vacant position the following Thursday, as though the decision had already been made.

But the decision had not been made at this time. I told him that if he did not get the position, this would be the first time I would confront failure for any of my predictions. I asked him to give me his home telephone number, in case I wanted to call him. He did so.

When the next Thursday morning arrived, I telephoned Roadway Express and asked to speak to the terminal's secretary, Bernice. I asker her, "Who got the sales representative job in Monroe?" Bernice replied, "Sam." I said, "Thank you," and hung up the telephone.

I immediately found Sam's home telephone number and dialed. He answered the phone and said, "You were right, Willie, in your prediction." I congratulated Sam again. "You see, Sam, I wanted to let you know in advance as a test of my continued ability to make predictions." I continued to prevail 100% without failure.

Traveling Miracle in Van

In 1997 and 1998, I had a part-time job as a stainless cookware salesman. My supervisor, Jerry, called on the telephone late in the evening, just before darkness. He asked me to meet him about halfway between my house in Williamston and Anderson. Jerry lived just on the far side of Anderson. He wanted to get some paperwork from me to turn in before I would see him again at the next weekly meeting.

I departed my home a little early so that I could stop by another place before meeting Jerry at a gas station on highway I-85. At night I wore eyeglasses when driving. En route to meet Jerry, my eyeglasses had fallen to the floor of the '95 Ford van that I was driving. I attempted to retrieve them. I wanted to have a clearer vision while I was driving. The road was not so familiar to me because I had not traveled it in quite some time.

In the process of retrieving my eyeglasses, I approached a stop sign that I really did not see until it was too late to stop. I was driving at a continuous speed about 40 miles per hour with no slow down as I approached the stop sign. There were three cars traveling the road to my left on the crossroad. They were approximately a car length apart and going in the same direction.

I realized that there was going to be a wreck, unless I could do something instantly. Running through the stop sign, my vehicle went in between the limited space between two of the cars without touching or even getting a scratch on any vehicle. I crossed a ditch and traveled into the yard of a resident heading straight. I came to a stop on the left side of the tree without touching it. I backed out of the yard and continued to travel on to meet my supervisor.

My supervisor and I met at the designated place on I-85 at the gas station. I was so excited at not having wrecked my van that I revealed to Jerry what had just happened moments earlier. I looked around my van and noticed that there was not any damage to the vehicle.

After returning home, I told my wife, Frances, about the miracle. All was well—no wreck, no injuries, and no damage to the vehicle. I continued to wonder afterwards how this happened.

Of course, the cars traveling on the crossroad probably were wondering what they saw when I crossed between them. It wasn't superman, but it was me guided by the hand of God.

It had to be a miracle I had just experienced. Thanks be to God for his miracles being performed.

Possible Severe Injury

The Lord works in mysterious ways. At Roadway early one morning, I was walking to the terminal yard from the parking lot. On this particular morning, the weather was foggy, making visibility very poor.

While walking about one-half way to the building terminal, one of the switch-tractors that move trailers from one place to another and to and from the dock was headed straight toward me at the regular speed in this foggy condition. At that moment, an accident seemed almost inevitable resulting in a switch-tractor hitting me. No telling what the consequences of that tragedy that would have been.

Thank God that Bobby, who was a regular switcher, was sitting in the tractor while an amateur driver was training and learning to drive the switch-tractor. The amateur driver did not see me walking in the heavy fog on the yard. An alert Bobby saw me and quickly diverted the tractor to avoid hitting or running over me, avoiding almost certain injury or maybe even death.

Thanks again to Bobby and God for preventing a disaster.

Incidentally, the exact time of this incident, the hour and minute, coincided with the time my sister, Cynthia, died a few months earlier in the Anderson Medical Center in Anderson, SC. This was something to think about in relation to her death and my avoidance of tragedy through Bobby and God.

Unbelievable Financial Offer

Hard times come on a financial basis. During the 1990s, a lack of sufficient money to pay bills was very evident. I had tried and wondered how to get enough money to bring my bills up to a current status. The mortgage on the house was past due and there was no money to pay it.

At one time, I actually gave up and said, "I hope the Lord will intervene and help me out financially." I could not see my house being foreclosed. I just started relaxing, stopped worrying, and believed by faith in the Lord that He would get me out of this financial situation.

A few days later, a mortgage lender called me and asked if I needed any money. I was surprised, but overjoyed. I told him the situation and then asked if they would loan me the money. If so, it would be greatly appreciated. The financial institution loaned the money to me.

Oh! What a big relief. It takes a strong belief and faith in the Lord that he can help you when you need it the most. Thanks be to the Lord.

Hospital Patient Condition

I have had many friends. One of my friends, Johnny, lived in the Five-Forks area of Anderson County His wife graduated with me in 1955 from Caroline High School in Williamston and he married a classmate of mine.

One night when Johnny was returning home, he had an accident in his car. The accident occurred not far from his home. He was transferred to the Anderson Medical Center in Anderson.

The news of this accident was revealed to my wife and me the night of the accident. We immediately got into our car and went directly to the hospital to see how Johnny was doing. The doctors said that he was in stable condition.

At the hospital, we were allowed to enter the room where Johnny was placed. Other family members and friends were there. We all talked at a minimum to Johnny, while he seemed to look at us during this time.

When I reached a place in the room where I could see Johnny and get his reaction, something came to me, telling me that Johnny would not make it, even though everyone else thought he would recover from his injuries.

Outside of the hospital, several people were in a huddle talking of Johnny's condition. They believed that he would make it out of the hospital. I told them I disagreed with their thoughts and that something told me that Johnny would not make it out of the hospital alive. I regretted to inform them of the sad news, which was the opposite of what they were saying.

My wife and I left the hospital and returned home that night. Shortly after returning home, a telephone call came and said that Johnny had just died. That moment of something coming into my mind and telling me what would happen meant that my predictions were continuing to prevail, regardless of the situation or time or regardless of where I might be.

Thanks be to God for instilling in me this power of His. I reminded the persons of what I told them about Johnny and they told me that I was right.

The Empty Chair

My brother-in-law, M. B. Porter, Jr. came by our house one day to visit my wife and me. At that particular time, we were living at 15 School Street in the town of Williamston. He borrowed my wife's car, with her permission, to drive that night.

After going to bed and falling asleep that night, I was awakened to hear the rocking of an empty chair in the den. It was the same chair in which Jr. was last sitting before leaving the house. I asked my wife, Frances, if she heard the chair rocking in the den. She replied that she did not hear the rocking.

The next morning, we were informed by an incoming telephone call that Jr. was involved in a wreck with the car. He was partially submerged in a creek just off Liberty Highway in Anderson. Someone passing in an automobile spotted the wreck off the highway. The car was only partially visible, due to brush and high weeds around the wreck area. Jr. was transported to the Anderson Area Medical Center in Anderson.

After visiting Jr. at the hospital and seeing him in bad condition, I told everyone that Jr. would be all right and would recover afterwards. This was an accident warning him to get right with God.

Later, Jr. improved and was dismissed from the hospital.

Examination Score

When I was teaching in the public schools during my early years of marriage, South Carolina teachers were paid compensation according to their score on the National Teachers Examination. During this particular time, I already had a grade of "B" on the examination, but I felt as though I could make an "A" on the exam.

One morning, on the scheduled day for the next National Teachers Examination test to be given in Greenville, I decided to take the test. On this particular morning during January, the weather was bad. It had snowed and sleeted the night before, making driving hazardous.

The distance to travel to take the test was 15 miles, from Williamston to Greenville. The road was covered with sleet, ice and snow. I was driving slowly, about 18 miles an hour, behind a greyhound bus leaving the town of Pelzer. All of a sudden, my car started veering to the left side of the highway. I wondered if there was a car or vehicle approaching from the opposite direction, because the bus in front of me obstructed my view of oncoming traffic. Luckily as I veered toward the left side of the road there was no vehicle approaching from the opposite direction.

Something came to me instantly in my mind and told me that the brakes on my car would not help me due to the fact of ice being on the road. That something told me to turn my steering wheel to the right, which would cause the back end of the vehicle to swirl around and bring my car to a stop. If it did not stop at the edge of the cliff in that manner, then I should immediately jump out or get out of the car somehow before it plunged down a steep embankment, thus trying to avoid serious injury.

I did that in about two or three seconds. My car swirled with the back end stopping at the edge of the cliff on the opposite side of the road. I got out of the car after coming to a complete halt, and saw that the back wheels of the vehicle were only about 2 feet from the edge of the cliff.

I did not get nervous because quick thinking that came to me on the spur of the moment prevented that from happening. I got back in my vehicle and headed toward Greenville to take the National Teachers Examination.

A little while later, while en route to Greenville, I started to get a little nervous thinking about what had happened that could have led to serious injury. After arriving in Greenville safely and on time that morning, I proceeded to take the examination. My performance and results were astonishing. I made an "A" on the exam, despite what I went through before the exam on that particular morning.

Thanks be to God who guides and makes the right decisions always.

Miracle in School Bathroom

I had been talking to some co-workers about the amazing and astonishing things that could happen and did happen at various places.

There was a bathroom near my classroom at the school where I taught Special Education. One day, Joyce, the custodian of the school came to see about the light in the bathroom. She said that she would have to replace that light because it had gotten dim and seemed to be burning out. So I decided to see if my presence under the light would make a difference or have an effect on the dimness of the bathroom light.

I walked into the bathroom and stood under the light. In a few seconds, the light became brighter and shone, as a new light would shine with brightness. At that moment, I called one of my co-workers to come and watch the light get brighter as I stood under it.

Amazement and astonishment overcame my co-workers. They witnessed the fact that I had some kind of influence on the light bulb when I stood under it. After I left the bathroom, the next person went into the bathroom. I asked them if the light was still shining brightly, as a normal light would. They told me that the light was okay.

When the custodian came back to fix or replace the light, I told her that it would not be necessary to replace the light because of the fact that it was working fine now. Of course, I told her the true story and she became amazed and astonished. More witnesses have seen things happen in my presence.

Specifics of a Personal Tragedy

Naturally, my dreams would come while sleeping, no matter whether it was day or night. On this particular night, I dreamed of a personal tragedy concerning a member of the family. I will not divulge the name due to personal respect and the specifics of the dream.

The next morning, someone I knew approached the screened porch of the house to relay some news to me. I already knew and could tell them the specifics without them telling me, because I had that dream the night before. The person that approached me was really astonished to find out that facts were in my dream.

In my dream, two of my children had been playing on top of an old car that was sitting in my parent's yard down the street. They were climbing up the front and sliding down the back of the car over and over, as if it were a sliding board. One of them accidentally slid down onto the tag of the car and was seriously injured, which required a stay in the hospital.

This was another dream that came to be true exactly the way it was to be.

Episodes at Three Restaurants

My wife and I, during our return from Louisiana, were visiting and traveling from place to place in my own vehicle. There are moments when it is time to eat, no matter whether it is breakfast, dinner, supper or simply a taste for something special, even if it's "gumbo" in the French or Pelican state known as "Louisiana."

On the way from New Orleans to Baton Rouge, we decided to stop at a restaurant. After entering the restaurant, we ordered. We waited patiently while our food was being prepared. All of a sudden, a waitress came out of the kitchen with the tray in her hand and she dropped the tray of food intended for us. The waitress said, "This is the first time that I have ever dropped a tray of food like this, but I will prepare another tray for you."

After the second tray was prepared, the waitress came out of the kitchen, this time without incident, and safely laid the tray on the table before us. She apologized for the incident. We told the waitress that everything was okay.

After we finished eating, we left and continued on the way to our destination of Baton Rouge. While on the way, we discussed the incident that happened at the restaurant we had just left.

During the next day in Louisiana, we stopped at another restaurant, this being a different one, to dine again. We placed our order with the waitress. She said, "It will not take a long time to prepare your order", and that she would return shortly.

As we sat at the table while our food was being prepared, we discussed what had happened at the previous restaurant, wondering and hoping that the same incident would not occur again this time.

The waitress came out of the kitchen with our food. About halfway coming to us, the waitress dropped the whole tray of food on the floor. This waitress, a different one from the previous, said to us, "I am sorry that I dropped your food. I don't understand it because I have never done this before since working as a waitress. You will be served another tray of food. Sorry about the incident."

The waitress went back into the kitchen. We discussed the similarity of circumstances occurring in different restaurants with different people. What a correlation that is happening wherever we go.

The waitress came out of the kitchen and placed the tray of food on our table, apologizing for what had happened to the previous tray of food. We enjoyed our second tray of food without incident.

Shortly, we decided to leave and continue our sightseeing of places and people in Louisiana. On the last day of the week in Louisiana, we were leaving New Orleans, where we had been staying not far from the Super Dome. We decided to stop at a restaurant in Slidell, Louisiana to eat our last meal in Louisiana. We stopped at a restaurant, one that we had never been to before.

After entering, we gave our order to the waitress. She then went into the kitchen to prepare our order of food. While waiting on our food, we discussed again what had happened to other waitresses in the other two restaurants. We wondered if it was possible that the same thing would occur for the third time at this restaurant.

The waitress came out of the kitchen. Halfway to us, this waitress dropped our tray of food that had been prepared. With astonishment, the waitress shook her head and said, "I cannot believe that I dropped this order of food. It has never happen to me. I just don't understand and don't want to believe that I dropped this tray of food. Sorry this happened. I will get your another tray of food."

While the waitress was in the kitchen, we could not believe that similar circumstances have happened in three different locations in Louisiana involving different people, unknown to each other.

The waitress returned with our food and was being extra careful. After we finished eating, we said it was time to keep moving out of Louisiana before a fourth similar incident would happen again for some reason.

It must have been something about me that triggered all three incidents. That is, some sort of radiance or something maybe like the lights coming on during my presence. Maybe, one day, the mystery of these occurrences, being so similar, will be researched.

As we continued traveling on our way home, back to the state of SC, there were not any more of these incidents happening, of which we were glad.

God in Control

In my later years at Roadway Express, Inc, in 1996, while working on the night shift, 10:30 pm to 7:00 am, my head seemed to be clogging or stopping up with something like a sinus infection. About the middle of my shift, I decided to take half of a medicine tablet that I saved in a bottle for some years because the tablet was so good. It had relieved me in about 2 hours from the same condition that I was feeling at this time.

I finished my shift and departed for home, a distance of 15 miles. About two miles from reaching home, I started to get real sleepy, while driving at the wheel of my pick up truck. I was battling to keep my eyes open on Highway 20, leading toward the town of Pelzer, SC. I suddenly went to sleep at the wheel of the truck while beginning to round a curve. My truck to travel, without me in control, down and around a steep curve before crossing the Saluda River Bridge, which separates Anderson County from Greenville County.

My truck continued traveling up the road approximately 1,000 yards, still with me asleep, before veering to the right side of the road. As it began to veer off the road in some high grass, my eyes began to open. I did not know my whereabouts on Highway 20. The only thing that came to my mind as I left the highway was the movie, "Twister", because of a similarity of high weeds and grass. In front of me, I could see a telephone pole. As I headed toward it, with a short distance to go before hitting it, there was no time to avoid an accident

A passing motorist saw me after the accident and called the rescue squad to take me to the Anderson Medical Center in Anderson. This motorist had a cellular phone from which to make the emergency call. I was fortunate. I had no broken bones. I did not collide with any on-coming vehicle traffic as I traveled along and around various curves going downhill. I crossed the bridge safely before coming to a stop at the telephone pole.

It was God who had control of my truck from the moment of going to sleep until colliding with the pole. The circumstances could have been worst. God made sure that everything was in His hands, that is, HE was the one and only one who drove the truck that distance. Every time that I would pass that section of highway, it would always amaze me how God can take control, making everything much better. I will always give credit to my God for taking care of me at all times.

The photo below is an aerial view of Route 20.

Our United States President

We have had several United States Presidents take office after winning political elections during my lifetime, including the present one, Barack Obama. Just continue reading what I'm going to say about one of them.

This particular president was Richard Nixon, who belonged to the Republican Party. Of course, party lines do not have anything to do with this writing.

It was during the "Watergate Scandal." The Senate Watergate Committee recessed early in August, after 37 days of televised hearings. On August 15, 1973, President Nixon, who had refused to testify, went on television to say, "Not only was I unaware to any cover-up, but . . . I was unaware of anything to cover up."

I happened to be in my bedroom at home the day that Richard Nixon appeared on national television, addressing the nation in a speech saying that he had nothing to do with or had no knowledge of anything about the Watergate scandal. As I looked into the president's eyes and face on TV, something came to me with a prediction at that particular moment saying, "Nixon is telling a lie. He might have some people or many people believing what he's saying, but not me."

I immediately went to the other room in the house where my wife, Frances, was and told her that Nixon just told the American people a lie, but not to me. I told her that he would do one of the following things soon while in office: (1) he would resign from office before the end of his term, or (2) he would be impeached from office before the end of his term as president. I told my wife to remember what I had told her because it is going to happen and that this was a prediction that will come true.

On July 24th, with more than a dozen of the President's former aides already sentenced for burglaries or for the knowledge of the cover-ups and payment of "hush" money, the US Supreme Court ruled unanimously that the president, Richard Nixon, must release the tapes. Between July 27th and 30th, the Judiciary Committee, after a month of hearings, voted to submit three articles of impeachment of the president to the full House. On August 2nd, subpoenaed tapes were delivered to Judge John Sirica. The tapes included the June 23, 1972 conversations, in which Richard Nixon and Haldeman had talked about using the CIA and FBI to present the Watergate break-in as a matter of national security.

Inside the White House, the President's lawyers called that tape "the smoking gun" proof that the President knew about the burglary and had set out to keep the facts from the government's own investigation. 18½ minutes of tape, "The Smoking Gun," with incrimination conversations, were erased from one of the White House tapes. On August 8, 1974, Richard Nixon went on TV to announce that he would resign the Office of United States President the next day at noon.

So Richard Nixon did my number one prediction, resign from office before being impeached. I told all of this to others before any of the proceedings were made known to the public. Oh! Thank you, God, for transmitting the future through me.

Dr Martin L King, Jr.

A teaching job in elementary education was offered to me at a school in Abbeville, SC, in the year 1968. Mendell, a co-worker from Williamston, also taught at this school. Both of us decided to take turns driving to work each day, since the school was a distance of about 40 miles from home one way. We thought that it would be better for us economically.

One morning during the middle of February 1968, while Mendell was driving to work, I told him that I had a dream before awakening that morning. On April 4th, 1968, a very tragic event would take place. When mentioning this to him that morning, it was almost 2 months later when this was supposed to take place. I wanted someone to remember what I predicted would happen.

When April 4th arrived, beginning that morning and throughout the workday, my dream of almost two months ago was on my mind, wondering if it would come true. At school then there were not any TVs or radios to watch or listen to like we have today. Nor were there any available for use nearby.

After returning home on April 4, 1968, as I entered into the house, I asked my wife if she had heard any unusual news that day. She said, "No". Of course, at that time, the TV was turned off and she was working in the kitchen preparing food. At that moment I said, "Okay". Then I immediately went to the den where the TV was and turned it on. After sitting in the rocking chair for a few moments, a "Breaking News Story" appeared on the TV. It said, "Dr Martin Luther King, Jr. was assassinated today in Memphis, Tennessee." I relayed the news to my wife in the kitchen and told her of my dream in February, even though it had to be tragic.

The Computer

The Internal Revenue Service of the United States Government is known by every American citizen who prepares and turns in an annual tax return.

It was for me, just before the April 15th deadline, to get H&R Block to prepare my tax return. My wife and I both entered the tax agency for preparation of forms to be mailed before the tax deadline.

The tax preparer, a lady, was sitting in front of her computer filling in the required figures and information when all of a sudden the computer started acting up and not working properly. The lady told us that this was the first time her computer had done something of this sort. She wondered what was going wrong.

At this particular moment, something came to me, saying that if I would go outside of the office for a brief period, like 2 or 3 minutes, then the computer would start functioning again like normal. This was happening because of the fact that I was standing beside the computer.

I immediately told her that I would step outside the door for a brief time and then return. After returning back inside the office, the lady said that the computer started back up as normal after I departed from the office.

After a few moments, I had realized that it was me and that something about me had affected the computer.

Lucky Dreams

While working at Roadway on the third shift, I would have to sleep in the daytime. One day during my sleep at home, I dreamed of driving my red Toyota pick-up truck. My trailer was attached behind the truck, loaded with trash and garbage going to the dump, which was about 5 miles from my home. In my dream, I drove to the dump and emptied my load at the disposal site.

On the way back home, there was a man standing in the middle of the road who flagged me to stop. So I stopped and wondered what the man wanted. He told me that he would like to buy my red truck. He had cash money in his pocket right then and he would pay me $10,000 for the truck.

At that moment, I started thinking very rapidly. I told him that, if he paid me the $10,000 right then, I would give him the empty trailer behind my truck also. I would be glad to walk the remaining two miles back home. After all, I could buy another truck later and still have some money left over. So the man paid me $10,000 in cash and I let him have the truck and trailer. Merrily, I walked the remaining distance home.

After awakening from my dream, something told me to play the tag number of that red truck in the lottery because that would be the winning number on the next day.

When I got off from work the next morning at 6:00 am, I started driving for about half a mile toward the retailer to put the winning number in. I changed my mind, because it was too early and I did not want to wait for the retailer to open. Because of my working hours at the time, I decided to wait until the next day so that I could get some sleep. The next day would have been my last day to work that week.

That next day, I went to put that special number, 878, in the lottery. I was startled to find out that it came out the previous day, the day on which I changed my mind, turned around, and went home.

My luck was destined for me, but I changed my mind. Anytime there was money involved in my dreams, a lucky number would always show up. There is something that shows reality in my dreams consistently. That something seems to be coming from God, who directs me toward reality and the truth. Thanks be to God for His guidance.

Deceased Giving Information

I had a very unusual dream about someone who had died a few years ago. That someone was my Aunt Gladys, who lived down the street from me when she was living in Williamston. In this dream, my aunt, who was deceased, called me on the telephone. After the telephone rang one or two times, I picked up the receiver. To my amazement, my aunt told me that she was just calling to tell me what the lucky 3-digit number would be in the lottery. I said, "Okay." She told me to play the number 016. I said, "Thank you very much," and proceeded to hang up the phone.

I thought much about this dream of mine. It never happened before in all my dreams that someone who is deceased would call me and tell me on the telephone what to do. Therefore, I went ahead and played the number 016 and, believe it or not, that was the correct winning number in the lottery.

God works in mysterious ways. All you have to do is have trust in Him, because He will guide you.

Execution of Dream

As previously mentioned about my dreams, another miracle of luck prevailed the next day after dreaming of being lucky. As you know, a person cannot win in the lottery unless a purchase is made.

The next morning I went to a convenience store. While there, my mind told me to purchase a ticket from one of the several different kinds of tickets. In order to see if my dream the night before would come true, I asked the store clerk to give me one ticket. She said, "Don't you want more than one ticket?" I replied, "I just want to purchase one ticket." She said, "Okay."

After leaving the store, when scratching off the ticket, there appeared a match and win for $5,000. I scratched off the next number on the ticket, and there was another win for another $2,500. I was so excited at what was happening, I rushed back into the store. The clerk said that I forgot to scratch off the other hidden number. So she scratched it off for me, and there was another win of $5,000. Another scratch off was for $2,500 on the same ticket. This made the winner of the jackpot for that particular game—a total of $15,000.

"Wow!" I exclaimed with excitement. God had instilled luck in me through a dream. Thanks be to God! I will always appreciate what God had done and will do for me.

On this occasion, as on others when luck was involved, I did not take advantage of the opportunities for my monetary gain.

One Morning at Home

Getting a good night's sleep in bed means so much to everyone. It was one morning at home when I awakened from my night's sleep. I arose and sat on the edge of my bed. Something came to me through my mind and told me that I would be lucky today. That something told me to go and play a Cash-5 ticket and the numbers would be my five children's birthdays. While sitting for a few moments and trying not to forget what was directed to me by that something, I wrote on paper the birthdays of our five children. Now I had to enter these numbers into the drawing to see whether that something which came to me would really be true.

During the day, I entered the five numbers in the drawing and waited at home for the results. Later the results were publicized. As I read the numbers, excitement began to instill in me because, as I read the numbers from left to right, the first number was correct, the second number was correct, the third number was correct. I then began to feel more excitement and tension building within me. The fourth number was correct. Could it be the jackpot for me? My eyes then read the fifth number, which was 38 instead of 28. I stared at the 38 and said, "Oh! How close can a person get?" I had already realized from my first four numbers that I was lucky, but also realized how close I was to winning the $250,000.

Thank you, God, for the monetary luck that I did win.

Before Going to the Beach

Many families get together at regular intervals, whether it be yearly, or every two years for what we normally call "family reunions." This occasion is anticipated and hopeful, a place designated where families get together for fellowship, excitement, fun and a chance to meet again or meet for the first time, thus getting better acquainted with especially close kindred.

On one day during the month of August, my family planned to travel to Myrtle Beach, SC to meet other families of close kindred for a family reunion. The night before leaving for the beach, I had a dream. This was a special dream, one that could make me a millionaire. Why? The Lottery Jackpot in New York had reached $100,000,000. I knew that, with having relatives in NY, it would only take a telephone call to them to put in my dream numbers before they departed for Myrtle Beach.

I dreamed of six lucky lottery numbers that I would relay to my family in NY, so that they could be entered in the drawing for me before they departed for the reunion.

Time continued to be a rush for me, getting ready and packing for departure. Well, we did depart for the beach, but I forgot one very important transaction—to call my family in NY to get my dream numbers entered in the next lottery drawing.

After arriving at the beach, I said that if my numbers did not come out in the drawing I would be happy. Why would I be happy? Yes, I would be very happy by not seeing my numbers drawn for $100,000,000 because I didn't get them entered in the lottery drawing. On the other hand, if my numbers came out in the drawing, then I would get a sickly feeling.

At the beach on the day of the drawing, which was televised, I decided to quietly get my pen and paper, sit in front of the TV, and record first hand the drawing results from NY (live). So that I did. And to my disbelief, my dream numbers were drawn for $100,000,000 in NY. I began to talk to others at the reunion about how I missed winning the NY lottery simply by my forgetting at a crucial moment before leaving home to make that special and important telephone call.

There were four persons who had identical and correct numbers for the drawing. Oh! I could have been the fifth person with the correct numbers. I could share the winnings to the tune of $20,000,000. It was my fault, because my lucky dream did come true even though I did not enter my dream in the lottery.

Thank you, God, for instilling in me those lucky dreams!

Attention from My Father

Going to bed to sleep a comfortable night of rest is the goal for most everyone. On this particular night at home, I got in bed as usual to relax and sleep.

Later in the night, after going to sleep, I was awakened by a plain voice coming from the direction of the church cemetery located within the same city block where I lived. This voice was clearly my father's, who has been deceased several years. The voice called me by name. I immediately asked my wife, who was sleeping, "Did you hear my father talking to me?" She said, "No." After all, she was asleep.

But the voice was directed to me, being loud and clear. This was a communication to me from my father, who rests in a grave not far away in the church cemetery. It is amazing to receive communication from the deceased. I will never forget this communication from my father.

In Late Hours of the Night

When people go to the medical doctor, he instructs them about what he expects the patient to do—follow instructions. I was instructed by the doctor to take a blood-pressure medicine on a daily schedule in order to regulate, or stabilize my blood pressure.

During one month, after taking the prescribed medicine, the medicine had been completely exhausted. So I decided to wait a few days, before getting my medicine refilled at the pharmacy.

In the middle of the night, while asleep, I suddenly woke up after what seemingly felt like a blood vessel in my head had burst. Then, suddenly at that moment, I got up out of the bed, turned on the lights, and rushed to the bathroom with the instant thought of hoping that blood would not come out of my mouth when spitting in the bathroom. When I spit, there was some blood coming out. I began to wonder what had happened to me, hoping it would not be serious. My thoughts told me that if I continued to see the presence of blood coming out of my mouth then I should go to the hospital as soon as possible. Well, the blood seemed to stop. I decided to take my blood pressure using my home kit. When taking my pressure, my bottom number registered higher than ever before.

I decided to go the doctor's office the next morning. After examining me at the office, he told me that it was a miracle that I did not have a stroke. He told me to never skip taking my blood pressure medicine. I agreed to what the doctor was instructing me to do.

This episode made me realize better the importance of obeying the doctor's instructions. It was God that prevented me from having a stroke and I thank Him for what He has done for me.

On a Rainy Day

One day, later in the afternoon, I had planned to cut grass in my yard, but just as I began, it started to rain. At that moment, something came to my mind telling me to go to the video store and play the machine, giving myself the opportunity to win some money. Maybe it would stop raining later and give me the opportunity to cut the grass.

The destination was only short distance from where I lived. So I went, sat down and started playing the machine. Shortly after being there, I hit the jackpot for $5,000.

This occurrence seemed like a dream, but it was reality. Thanks be to God for guiding my mind to do what would be beneficial to me financially. If it had not rained, I would not have won the jackpot. Many times when my mind tells me to do something, it would always come true.

A Way Provided by God

One morning, when I was driving home from work at Roadway Express, there were things that came across my mind, such as wondering where I could borrow $200 until payday. I needed to pay a telephone bill that was due.

About 5 miles from home I thought of stopping by a Quick Stop store where there was a person I knew who might lend me the money until payday, which would have been that weekend. He, the manager of the store, told me that he did not have that amount that morning.

Something came to my mind. I knew that I had only one dollar in my pocket. There were video machines in his place of business, I followed my mind to play one of the video machines and see if it would make me lucky to get the money I needed. So I put the $1 in the machine and it immediately lit up, because I hit for $200, just like that. So I received $200, which I did not have to pay back to anyone.

It is amazing how things would come to me and be true. Thanks to the ALMIGHTY GOD for leading me at all times.

Unexpected Win

On a nice summer day, I was driving from my home in Anderson. I had purchased this home in 1999, after retiring from 27 years at Roadway. As I traveled toward my previous hometown of Williamston, my vehicle radio was tuned to station WRIX, 103.1, in Anderson. At the time, this was one of my favorite radio stations.

The radio announcer was asking a question for anyone in radio land to answer. If the correct answer was given, then the caller would win a prize. The question was "What is the name of a famous German scientist who surrendered to the United States Army in 1945 and later worked on guided missile systems for the US Government?"

I had written the telephone number of the radio station on a piece of paper and placed in front of me near the dials on my truck, so that if anytime I needed or had to call this radio station for anything, the phone number would be handy.

When this particular question was asked, I took out my cell phone and dialed the station, hoping that no one else would get ahead of me with the answer to the question. All of a sudden, the radio announcer asked me what the correct answer was. I told him that the German scientist's name was Wernher Von Braun. The announcer immediately said, "You are absolutely right. Your prize will be waiting for you at the radio station."

Instant reaction was the key applied that had successful results on this particular summer day.

Dream Directions

When a person goes to bed and falls asleep for the night, he does not know what dream might occur. When he awakens afterward, he may remember it.

One night I went to bed for a relaxing rest after working during the day. When I awakened the next morning, my dream during the night was very clear and precise. In this dream, I was told what to do to be lucky and where to go.

My lucky number would be found at a certain place in Baton Rouge, Louisiana. I should telephone my cousin in Baton Rouge and tell her to go outside her house and write down the tag number on her car that was sitting in the driveway. After doing this, she should return to the telephone and give me that number.

I followed my dream directions. My cousin did exactly as I told her. She asked me why I wanted to know this number. I replied that the reason was to follow my dream and see if the number would be lucky in the lottery. I thanked my cousin. After all, I was living in South Carolina while she was living in Louisiana. Therefore, I had to ask her for this information on the telephone.

I immediately played this number in the lottery Pick-Three. It was the lucky number that day.

This was another example of my following and doing exactly what my dreams tell me to do. The Lord works through me in various ways with dreams and predictions that always come true.

Wrapper at Store

There are things that persons would or would not believe. The unbelievers become believers simply by witnessing true events when they occur.

After awakening one morning, I remembered a dream that developed during the night. It told me to follow specific directions in order to be lucky.

The dream told me to go to the store and purchase one honey bun. After purchasing this food item, I was to look at a certain place on the wrapper where I would find a number. I should play this number in the lottery and I would be lucky.

So I did exactly as the dream told me. Would you believe the results? The number on that honey bun wrapper was the lucky number.

Well, I did not eat the honey bun, but only bought it at the store to see if my dream would come true. The only thing I wanted was the specific lucky number on the wrapper of that honey bun.

God continues to guide and direct me to specifics, no matter where the specifics might be. I give thanks to Him.

Television Show

Many people watch television. Of course, there is a variety of programs and shows are to be seen by choices made by a person tuning in selected channels on the television.

When I was sitting in the den at home with my family and others, a particular show was on. It was very interesting to us on this particular night. The name of the show was 'The Price Is Right'. The announcer had a lady standing near him and a brand new car was sitting near, in sight. The announcer told the lady that, if she could guess the price of the vehicle, she would win the car.

Something came to me then and I knew that the lady would not guess the correct price, but if I were on the show, my answer would be correct, thus winning the car. That something gave me the answer.

I told my family and the others about my wishing to be on the show. So, they should listen carefully and watch the show to see who had the correct answer. I told everybody what the correct price would be for that brand new car. We all waited patiently and attentively.

The lady on the show gave her answer, but it was wrong. The announcer told her the correct price, which was exactly the price that was told to me moments before by that something, $7,498.00.

I immediately arose out of my seat on the couch and exclaimed that, if only I had been on that TV show, I would have won the nice new vehicle. All around said that my price was right, to the dollar.

I have always said, and others have said also, that I have a special gift in predicting ever since I was about six years old. This gift continues to prevail, even to the present day, as you read this book. Remember, I don't seek the future, but the future comes to me by that something at any time or any place with 100% accuracy.

Little League Football Game

The day was ordinary, with the exception of what was to transpire later in the evening. My grandson, Dustin, was an eight year old football player who played with a local team in Pelzer, SC. This football team had a scheduled game to play in Belton, SC.

Families and others associated with or connected to the football players would follow and support the players when they were scheduled to play, whether at home or away. This meant a lot to the young players, knowing they were supported by home folks.

It was on a Friday during football season when our family traveled to Belton, only a few miles away, to see our grandson play in the game as a running back with the team. I was standing on the sidelines during the fourth quarter of the game, with only a few moments remaining. The opposing team was leading by a small margin. Something came to me and I knew that, on the next play of the game, a player on our team would get the ball and run all the way down the football field for a touchdown and we would win the game.

You see, I was foretold what would happen near the end of the game. This prediction of mine, given to me by that something, was precise and with the accuracy that has been, and continues to be, amazing. No matter where I might be or what time it might be, it is always before the happening.

The Night Before

There are many things that can occur during the night. It was in December of 2009 when I had a dream during the night. It showed me that soon there would be a change in my position as an assistant teacher at the high school in Williamston, SC, where I worked with others in Special Education. The dream told me that I would be called into the principal's office and be reassigned to another position in the school.

Well, on Friday, December 4, 2009, at approximately 2:00 p.m., the teacher with whom I worked informed me that the principal at the school wanted to see me in the office at 2:30. I immediately wondered why I was being called to the office on, seemingly, the spur of the moment. My mind referred me quickly to my dream the night before, which was on Thursday, December 3.

After arriving in the office at 2:30 to meet with the principal of the high school, I was informed by him that he had a re-assignment for me. It was to begin Monday, December 7, in another phase of Special Education at the school. I would be assigned to a special student who would be transferred to a different section in the school on that date.

My dream of the night before came true. It is amazing how true things to be come to me by way of dreams. It is not by dreams alone, but by that something informing me in predictions of what to expect as well as answers.

Instant Prophecy From God

One morning I had to go and take care of some business in Anderson, sometimes referred to as the Electric City. Something came to me from God telling of a Cash-Four number that was going to come out in the South Carolina Lottery that day and that it would play exactly as told. That number was 8338. After thinking for a moment about my past realizations coming true, I decided to play that particular number exactly as that something told me, that it would be in the midday drawing. So I followed through to see if this prediction would come true as many other predictions in the past have come true.

On returning home from my business trip to Anderson that afternoon following the midday drawing, I searched the results for that particular lottery. To my amazement, joy, and happiness, I realized again that miracles are real, the ones that God is the instigator of, and how He goes about performing these miracles. Yes, 8338 was the correct number in the Cash-Four drawing for the State of South Carolina.

This joy and feeling of happiness that God gave me was a wonderful feeling that you can only imagine. During this bad economic time in America, this was a nice gift from God that benefitted me financially. I thank You, God, for what you have done for me.

To claim the prize, I had to make a special trip to Columbia because of the amount and because of the law in South Carolina governing the limit over which local merchants are not allowed to pay. The next day, I planned a trip to Columbia in the morning hours, arriving there when the claims office opened for business. As a matter of fact, I was the first customer to arrive at the office that morning.

After being at the claims office for a few minutes, a lady from another part of South Carolina entered, evidently to claim her winnings. Something came to me instantly after her arrival that told me to ask her about her winning. That something told me that she was going to cash in on the identical number, Cash-Four 8338, that I had myself. Now, remember that there are many different numbers that could come on during the same day. Therefore, after briefly talking with her in the office, I asked, "What was your winning number?" She answered, "8338." I then congratulated her, knowing what her number was before she told me. This was due to the fact that something from God came to me before the results were made known.

God is good and He does wonderful works. You have to trust and believe in Him and know that He is good. God gave me that gift ever since I was six years old when I was confronted by a 'ghost' as told in the first section of this book. The gift continues to prevail in various ways and continues to come true, all the times before and now. Thanks be to God for this true gift.

The Unknown Tag

A member of my family, after graduating from a well-known university in South Carolina, traveled to Georgia to find a job in the area of her degree. After finding a job and moving to Georgia, a car tag from the state of Georgia had to be displayed on her vehicle because of residency requirements.

While visiting back home on a weekend, something told me to ask her to call and let me know the new tag number. But, for some reason, she forgot to call. Without knowing the new tag number, something came to me that a certain tag number would be her lucky number. This took place on the morning of July 9, 2011. When the midday lottery results came, it was 321, her number. A few days later, she came home and visited the family. One of the first things I noticed on her car tag was the number that came out in the South Carolina lottery.

Can you imagine me predicting the new number on her car tag which I had never seen or heard of before? It was through God's informing me of a miracle being performed. God has a unique way of translating to me the unknown and releasing the truth to be sought. Without Him, things would not be the same. Have trust and believe in Him daily because God has wonders to perform.

That Car

After retiring from my job, where I worked for 27 years, my wife and I traveled around to various places in Anderson County, South Carolina looking for the ideal house in which we wanted to live as two retired persons. This was one of our objectives in life following retirement.

As the days passed and after seeing many new homes, we decided to purchase a house that was more ideal for us than any others we saw during our phase of searching for a new home.

One day, a car that had never been driven to our new home entered the driveway. Something told me that the tag number on that vehicle would be the correct number coming out in the lottery within the next 24 hours. After thinking about that something, I decided to follow up by searching the next 24 hour results to verify whether it was true.

Believe it or not, that number actually was the winning number, as predicted and instilled in me by translation from God. It gave me a unique feeling of what God can do.

After thinking about the situation, I gave God praises for what He had translated to me. Thanks be to God because He has the credit and ways of doing marvelous things through human beings here on earth.

Editor's Note

While working on this book, my computer mysteriously starting slowing down. Eventually, I had to reinstall the operating system and all software.

When I was ready to finish the final version, half of my files were gone. Fortunately, I had saved the original CD that Mr. Wright's daughter had provided, and was able to continue.

During the time we were working together, Mr. Wright had often been near my computer. Coincidences or connections?

Thanks to:

My daughter, Anita Blassingame, typist

Adamene Robinson, editor

Shelby and William Allen, supporters of this book

David Rogers, picture

Thomas Addison, artist

Others who witnessed the true stories in this book

All illustrations were drawn by Thomas Addison.

Photographs are from Mr. Wright's collection.

About the Author

Willie Wright, Sr. was born in upstate South Carolina before World War II. His parents are Willie and Sadie Wright.

Willie began his education in First Grade at Caroline Elementary School, and went on to Caroline High School, where he graduated in 1955. He graduated from Southern University in Baton Rouge, Louisiana in 1959 with a B.A. degree in secondary education. While in college, he was a newspaper reporter for the university's 'The Digest'.

After returning to South Carolina, he pursued his education further by working toward a Master's degree at Furman University in Greenville, South Carolina, University of South Carolina in Columbia, South Carolina, and South Carolina State College in Orangeburg, South Carolina. He received an elementary teaching certificate to teach in South Carolina.

Willie has taught in upstate South Carolina elementary and secondary public schools for eighteen years. He has been a writer for 'The Williamston Journal' newspaper for the past eleven years. Willie retired from Roadway Express, Inc., after working there for twenty-seven years.

Willie has a wonderful wife, four children, and four grandchildren. He also has one brother and one sister.